To Cheri Fein

THE DAILY NEWS

by

BRAD GOOCH

Z PRESS

CALAIS · VERMONT

1977

Edited by Kenward Elmslie

Cover by Joe Brainard

The publication of this book was made possible by a grant from the
National Endowment for the Arts in Washington, D.C., a Federal agency.

Contents

The Silent Era

I haven't heard your name in a long time.
But I finally met someone just like you
who (helped by the after-image) looks fine.
Montage=Experience. The two
create an effect of life on a screen.
I bicycle across the flat, well-lit beach
where we met, attracted to each other's scene.
This is not a universal statement.
Just then a hand moves softly on my back
next it digs in and begins to massage.
I picture a river, an Indian attack,
the bright silver walls of a fuselage.
I first saw these pictures when I was with you, kid.
Now they're the same but on a different grid.

The Train Station

I want to go with you to some other place
which is more invisible, or if not that,
at least other-worldly. The train displaces
all our small talk with its straight monody
like a phone ringing for the umpteenth time.
Caught between channels on the Sears TV
we stand in the rain until it is time.
Your face dissolves immediately.
Just then the plants take on a grey and living buzz.
Where are you? Do you still like me like this?
These silly voices keep me up at night
as the snapshot on the dresser starts
to lose particularity. Across the street
you wave good-bye to me with fading feet.

Getting to Sleep

The clouds fell down to the ground and re-grouped
as snow. Pale and intense a figure walked
unhassled in the air. This documentary proves
that most men have dynamite eyes, hooked
up some way to silver box kites floating breezily
over an obsidian lake. On it a boat
supporting two thinking men skulks away.
I watched your beard grow while we were afloat.
I stood in front of the plate glass window
devising new tricks to do with my voice:
here a mirror, there a pair of engineer's boots.
At first the room seemed brightly lit in keeping
with our cowardly habits. Then your face
strobed in and out of view at an unconscious pace.

Rain

It's a silver afternoon in the Susquehanna.
On this new scale, my house becomes more important.
From the second-floor window, a mania
for beads knocks down the latent

good boy in all of us. The football
is under the influence of the planets, too.
There's no way to stop a rainfall
that expands from its brown shoes.

The 1930's was a brown decade.
We dressed in brown suits. Every street
led past an art deco arcade
under which a vibrating mother left her feet

in the scrapbook. In the middle of an open field
the girl with red hair comes to get laid.
Who says this funeral (my first) is sad?
Who gets the plaid bed where my grandfather dropped out of sight?

Don't be afraid of those little birds,
it's only the rain, made to keep you inside.
It's a window pressed against the mouth of dirty words
we say with our lips. At night the bride

turns into a fat, black bird.
She has lost her innovative raincap
on the bedsheet of the sky. Unfurled,
she spills a bright roadmap.

It's warm on the beach. You're awake as always
watching me come from the church on to the road.
A bird opens its wing. A mannequin displays
her secret eyes. A Buster Brown shoe erodes

beyond the elevator, into that blue shaft
where we move (evenly) like a train
within its tracks. What spring draft
brings these hypotheses to a weightless brain?

1. The softball has come down on my stagnant head.
2. Who was that you were with at the ballet?
And without leaving your kitchen, I obey the voice:
This lilac will be your breakfast instead.

From 3 until 10 in the Morning

The first thing that I noticed were your eyes
I was dancing with Bob, you were dancing
with a short guy in a tapestried shirt
but we were looking at each other. Five minutes
later I got away to go to the bathroom.
When I came back I sat down next to you.

We tried to figure out where I'd met you
But I didn't care, you seemed to care more. Your eyes
looked Spanish: Basque from Northern Spain. Your dancing
was geometric like mine, I thought you copied. Your shirt
was Brooks Brothers, or maybe Arrow, and in a few minutes
you opened it on a white T-shirt. The bathroom

downstairs was pedestrian, lonely. The bathroom
at my house can be lonely, too, but you
or anybody who'll look me in the eyes
and has nice eyes himself helps out. The dancing
changed from exercise to excuse, our shirts
were open, tails out. Telegraphic minutes

and the light gets our faces together, but in minutes
the dance is a teen-age leftover. By way of the bathroom
we get our coats. I want to get older with you
but not sleep with you yet. At the West End your eyes
keep steady, not unbalanced by love, but dancing.
This means you've made room for love before. Your shirt

(put on this morning) is an opera manager's shirt
or the shirt of a beginner who, in minutes,
tells me he sings too. On the way to the bathroom
I see your Vassar student ID. You
had shorter hair, or longer. Now your eyes
are surrounded by curly hair. Like two people dancing

in a forest opening, or not dancing
but standing far apart, staring. Your T-shirt
would be warm around me right now, the minutes
(the four hours) since you went to the bathroom
this morning, then left (I asked you to) made you
a solution to a lonely day. In my mind's eye

I see the uncomplicated minutes, next to you.
The outside light is on your dancing shirt
different from the bathroom light, my red eyes in the mirror.

Have a Good Adventure

I'd recognize that voice anywhere
Your hands
Your warm body
We wake up together on a cold morning
somewhere near Danbury, Connecticut
You're up a few hours before me
Already involved
We're asleep together
all day long
It's too late
to have a French romance
It's too late
to look for peace & quiet
in the woods
I close the two bedroom doors
Face the desk lamp
into the corner
One high note, a buzz
to the left and right of us
To know that activity is going on
which doesn't require us for its life
Our love doesn't always need us
One night you're down
I help you up
The next night I'm down
You help me up
But when we're both down
Our love goes on unconcernedly
So we have discovered something
the way a TV antenna discovers a channel.

The recipe
You make French bread
find Norwegian fortune-telling dice called "runes"
play Pichinko
or I play Pichinko
Cocteau at his desk
il pleut—I translate the poem
a tear-jerker but scientific
funny picture of Einstein getting ready
to take his nap in an old Vanity Fair
                          The elements
The rain is imagined to come down
When it is really coming down
or when (by force of mental inertia)
we think it's still coming down
There'll be good days There'll be bad days
There'll be days to make dinner together
And days when I type and you make dinner
Balinese dance days, Steve Reich trance days
Clever, sad, prayerful, erotic, battle-days
Days and nights, nights and long sleepy days
Days restless days balm-in-Gilead days.

Believe me when I say
I love you today and always
I even know it
sitting on the couch
when I can't stand being
next to you
that an exciting conversion
of heart and muscle
will send me into you

When I'm not there
Neither are you
which I don't regret
erratic as a star
socio-economico-environmentally determined
as the theory of quantums
I am in of and out of time
with and without you
but always near you
whoever you are
I can't get rid of you
as the world can't get rid of peace
for all its wars
Germany can't get rid of an old tune
"das kommt mir nicht aus dem Sinn".

Praise the Lord
Not for each event so much
as for the whole Rose of events
I look inside
wanting to sleep inside
the warm hallways and tunnels
of the Rose red on the outside
black on the inside with tiny lights
like stars, or bugs, crawling around
a circular staircase down down
into the ground. I've got your sound
in the ear of my heart
When you see something ("it's like haiku")
and tell me. Tell me something
about yourself I don't know
which is everything except your past

your hopes for the future
your opinions on this and that
Your eye is like a light blue rose
Where each spiritual fact is recorded,
even the fact of leaving,
or suffocating, or pushing away.

Nude

A gray flower
made of wire and soft paper
is touched by a tiny match
held in my hands
the sky is a watch
the minute hand slices
a cloud in two
on its way to 1
the magic number
of flowers grows
in a song
the gray flower dies
of a stem disease
cars span the distances
taking my voice to you
surrounded by a long body
with few weeks old beard
daddy is a sleepy house
mom shakes the earth
when she walks
from planet to planet
with her wooden plank
I walk the plank
in a striped suit
the nude boy
plays basketball
in high school
later in the morning
he will get up
covered in a light
that is really in my heart

turning and turning
the flame goes around
the gas burner
ready to support the soup
with its hot waves
recording each word
they say to one another
and what it means
in the life of the bed
which is a piazza
among the many streets and hours
that lead in and out of bed
I snooze past the anxious hours
into the really mad hours
Now you goddamned idiot
get out and dont come back
until youve found a job
and love me impersonally
the way you loved that starfish
for simply being on the beach
in a paralyzed state
under the sun, over the sand
and then I'll take you in
through the stomach
up the elevator to the light
of the eyes shining over our city
like car headlights on a parking deck

A dome of shiny met

A dome of shiny metal octagons
lowered by cranes
into the center city shopping mall
to provide rain protection
for the thin, pencil-line looking people
moving in a pattern below
My parachute is left hanging in air without me
walking on the wing of the plane above
doing scissor jumps
into the thin air not much oxygen
a gray day. The salt shaker
sketched alone on the canvas
like a bleak window

A skirt of cars continues to circle the city
coming and going, AM radios turned up loud
in the suburbs, cars have shopping bags inside
Here some cars have briefcases, or papers
not many bags. They go to New Jersey and Connecticut
where the supermarkets are bigger and easier to shop at
because of wide, sonorous parking lots
a few cars here and there, 24-hour shopping mart
the check-out ladies seem a little tired
One man at the fruit counter thinking about his friends
who have already died. The D-sharp light hits your eyes
like printing on a cash register stub
you wander around the aisles, looking for artichoke hearts
which they don't carry. Only beauty will save the world,
says Dostoevsky, who walked on White Nights
in St. Petersburg; his delicate soul is a little bird
that can be eaten in one bite, bones and all.

Turning down the dark street to go home
a warm feeling is already beginning. Soft sneakers
on grass, then on sidewalk, then on grass again
Buying candy and eating it, watching TV after supper
glad to be a dumb cowboy who drives a Buick out West
the sound of horses and cars together. The dog
has to stay off the furniture and out of the living room
So she hangs on, a sad idiot mongoloid baby
wrapped up in a cape with an umbrella next to her
The eyes reflect the flash of the camera
and now she's dead. I can think about her
feeling warm, sad . . . looking at birds
looking at hygiene books, hearing voices outside
trying to learn football for a year then giving up
and moving inside. Each one of us is sad.
Snowflake is sad she can't lay on the furniture.
Mom is sad to be married to my father
and not have many friends because my father is anti-social.
She tells me about his family while she cleans up
with a vacuum cleaner. Always cleaning. Sad.
My father is sad because he's worried about his job
and feels that my mother and I are a tight unit
and don't really like him, but he has to live with us
and go to work so we can eat. It's sad because the house is big
and I don't have many friends and don't stand up to bullies
and don't have anyone to talk to about Shakespeare
whose plays I imitate. A prince always kills a king.
I read the plays to my parents on the back porch
They ask me to go over to Fiaskis and play
I ask them why they don't have any friends either.
My dad gets angry but he's really hurt. I know
how to detect his sensitive parts. His psychological test
says he's an imaginative man and very shy and hard.

He has a big fantasy life
His affair with the secretary
was probably 50% fantasy. My mother
calls up the girl's mother and tells her.
Her mother was very upset
and if the girl really cared for my father
then my mother did a cruel thing
to get back at my father for marrying her,
or asking her to come back after the separation
when I was 3 years old, sitting on Nana's floor
waiting for them to get back from Ocean City
where my mother got a concussion on the dashboard
on the pull-up bridge. I blame my father
and think he did it on purpose, maybe unconsciously
he screams at night from dreams
especially after my grandfather dies
he's the only one at the nursing home
during these last hours, what's going on in his head
I confuse my grandfather's death with the death
of the grandfather on *Lassie*. A special half-hour show
makes him die on TV even though he had already died
in real life. They show him in a blurry heaven
in a rocking chair talking to his wife. When my mother's mother
died she said she saw my grandfather coming to take her away.

Opinion

Something like the Middle Ages is coming back. Monasteries are smarter than communes with rules worked out to prevent not cause problems. The Cistercians (trappists) should think about regrouping in space stations. Space is the modern equivalent of North African deserts. The monody of computer music is the modern equivalent of Gregorian chants. Psychology is most like the weather and least like a secret bureaucracy of id and ego. Thomas Aquinas' psychology makes more sense than Freud's and is more precise tho $X=$ angels and $Y=$ devils, that is, the words stop us short. What was the frame is now between channels: the patterns of gray space. Cocaine $=$ Paris, white and spacy. Acid $=$ New York, mental and fast, invigorating. The meditative poets of the 16th cent are back. A conceit is a metaphor, but from the opposite side of the brain. Prayer is exercise. Memory should be kept in spite of memory banks. The color of the seventies is gray, with silver a close second. Icon: blackboard. Word: invisibility. Language is the big issue for environmentalists, trees are secondary tho definitely there. Important to speak with sinuous or alive words (something like first ideas on Rhetoric) in order to preserve the planet. What you say turns into a wave which turns into the furniture (eventually) on which you sit. The only symbolic 1:1 language is the world. Any thinking which leaves out a part of the world (as math does to verbs and AJ Ayer to church hymnals) was invented to shut out rather than include the world. The mind is not a hat. The day is Mozart. The night is music to dance to.

The Sunset Years

Year of graduation, age, Long Island
nursing home, Pearl White tooth drops,
symptoms of second stage gonorrhea, juice
bar, disco engineer, tape deck, concentration
camp, cage, refrigerator murders, ice pics,
water pic toothbrush, injections, enema,
sound level, sex photo exchange, water boiler,
Con Ed bill, crabs, venereal warts,
prescriptions, Rx, the Daily News, the Hearst case,
using plants for fuel, Alger Hiss
typewriter, oxygen tent, last rites,
urine sample, water mark, postage due,
formaldehyde, freezing rain, black lung,
the diamond industry, PR, Haitian, Philipino,
9th Ave. and 38th St., floor-through, fire
house, rubber toys, classifieds, liquid
poppers, truth serum, lie detector test,
electric chair, court rulings, slicked back,
steamers, dust bowl, mix-o-matic, wart
remover, back porch thermometer, thermos,
sink stopper, lice remover, masseur, shower
head, dry cleaning, sine cosine, infrared,
comp time, happy hour, germs, arms
build-up, security risk, dash, anemic,
electric fence, polio vaccination, home
entertainment unit, the salt mines, dips-in-road,
battery-charger, price tag, bent, credit
card, escort service, chair, Moonlight
Drive-In, bargain basement, herbes, bomb scare,
court house, chasuble, crew-cut, dildo, store-
bought, close-up, high power lens, nerve gas,

Lincoln Continental, ocean waves, lunar eclipse,
ship grave, beep beep, late night, tax shelter,
antennae, radioactive fallout, pacemaker,
low blood pressure, sensitive instrument, dog tags,
sterile, manic, water meter, low-cal, on tap,
tie and jacket, cum stains, stopped-up drain, answering service,
sob story, limo, sinecure, tax deduction, opera buff,
cocktease, Francophile, tar and nicotine content, jazz,
deep end, other worldly, in like Flynn, pissed off,
hot under the collar, raking it all in, dristan,
space heater, feeder stream, spelling it out,
gadgetry, surface tension, litigation
proceedings, noise level, audiometer,
postal service, book rate, stamp
machine, $5 minimum, contact high.

Starve

The frozen fields
tracks of bison
and dinosaur
elephantine clouds
clobber overhead
the sky mops
endlessness
oh weary of life
days
smeared with life
nights
in an old tent
bones aching
damp
jammed
old lady Evans'
light still on
crude dreams
to the shower
in his sleep
lonesome
because before history
a giant's thumb
smell of printing ink
runs down the mountains
deep gullies and trails
bent-back trees
so big and black
the deep ponds boil
in heat
& change

deranged prairie dogs
yelp
run in packs
in the quick forest
wind and leftover
twigs stones
toenail
open-eared caves
and lakes
lucid pink rabbits
slouched dead
tired
on the inland rocks
turnips and hot
big flowers
right in her face
in the Stone Age

Riddle

It's my soul
I really care about
her
sheet metal
widening out in strips
to become a lake
bright with sun
rocks at the edges
different small fish
flick around inside
as water is to air
so are eyes and hair
to the soul
the world is made of water
shower water falls lightly
on the angel's back
which she scrubs
with her round brush
the musical fruit
is eaten winsomely
by three old men
no visible sign
but a tremor in the buildings
shakes windows apart
cops are on the scene
tons of radioactivity
carry sounds in the air
the Japanese night
on the street, listening
the bomb drops
a pink bulb is exposed

in blue, leafy nightlight
taste of soft cookies
in the new pantry
on the new block
friendless and solidifying
like a swingset
in the backyard
in winter
or a rock
consolidated headache-like
by Scotch and unhappy
recurring patterns
father-son teacher-student
Dad brings home a toy car
and bounces it in my lap
a terrible memory
because I love him
there
a storm
closes in on the two figures
older man and young kid
walking to an erased
building
to buy cigarettes

Words to be Broadcast over Eagle's Nest Sound System—I

Made out under sharp leg knife telephone golden shower boy under pinned under sweat sweet drill drilling broken glass smell faint smell aroma of needle tight bod no more but he kept going the slate eyes fastened on my boots tender touch Bud cop sweet and wet soaking the rub laying there time AM radio bondage songs out of touch brought back hard in the nose in the legs first the socks tight screwing into the ground tight tree phosphorescent beer too much too much a soft boy's voice beard hair arms legs loose and flowing fast down 18th Street at every corner mouth wet motorcycle cop glasses long to the knees hot and heavy you make me a pleasure machine a pleasure machine in the night you left me on the street to take a leak the dynamite sounds juke box still in my head my head knocked against that wall wet smelling one guy after another too much head hair cut off by your one hand the other leg stretched out body you've got it the tender touch in the palm of my hand in the insides of your legs your spell is tying me up in the stomach in the cock your hands keep moving in and out a heart a fist a piece of my heart goes with it and I've got you on the list starmaker bright gloves wristwatch try me piece of glass stuck in the heart a needle in my arm you've got the power to turn on the gas the electricity playing dead gun smoke your den my ass red tied into the socket dying to get you under my skin liquid popper scat b/m w/s Long Island master looking for expert slave meet at Interstate blacking out blacking one eye eye patch no leg Vietnam veteran marine action pow action muddy boots taken care of ready now to take what you've got giving you what's good for you taking you out on the street you dirty son of a bitch trigger happy in it for the action I never wanted to hear that phone voice again when he said to come drumming in the heart pumping slumping over on the sidewalk moonlight carlight headlight sideview walking down the street in front behind jewelry sounds my ear is in my head smell you robin fly fly robin fly right up to the sky pinned underneath heavy builder shit house rubber slit up the arm try to get away long day at work waiting to get home to my boy make him eat it blonde boy beard man extra money stay for a day in service in the tight bathroom for three days no way zinc gold spray today the day bars are full the gay bars are full I met him in the hall tall black cowboy no face under the hat sat on his boot ready to shine to shine skin wet ready dogs eyes ready no room two more and keep going until I say

Words to be Broadcast over Eagle's Nest Sound System—II

Big night two of them locked into by master lock service fifth floor walkup biceps tight across the face a little blood mostly follow me hot and sturdy masculine appearing stud stallion beat you into the ground tied to your leg tied to your bed forced to drink it soft and wet down the throat smell my scummy feet my BO take it and jack it off meeting in the bar on the pier hot sun body sunglasses no words straight to business businessman's shoes under the wheels covered in black grease in paint marked up shipped out drinking beer steady diet steady trucks moon pissing in the corner arc slap him silly the faggot match light reflected bootlight metal popper light covered over barlight starlight slapped over skinlight down on those socks around the room on all fours one after the other shoved down on hour ass in that corner Arab guy black guy white cowboy black minister master bible-carrying horny and ready to give in to your wishes sir the door locked from the outside guys watching you do it to it steady in pushing in soft then hard jackhammer machine gun soft then hard fist size bulletproof asshole ready to stop you keep me goin all day long no song jazz FM radio head music start late afternoon on the boots clean up wash socks apartment going deeper total washout in piss shit spit on me spit in the mouth piss in the mouth rolling around wet you've gotta make me play lose a day one eye one day at a time into handcuffs rope no mercy wrists tied out tied up outside left out all night cold and wet guys walk by cigarette burns in the nerves gone white I'm nothin but a worm turn on the amps let me burn dark hood sharp cut up scissors around the balls medicine man jabs inside make him cry can't breathe sock stuck down the throat dirt tongue shit covered new marks the ass the muscle front arms just waiting for your call roll over dog whore throat lick the floor got more silver vice visor execution man not movin hell down into your neck white neck never felt a mans boot never had a man pin you down hold back your shitty face and swallow tight bullets poison drinker mood elevator master in shiny pants policeman strict and ready to whip your act up ass boy cell block electric chair in veins shot of something straight into heart I pull the strings and you do the dance socksucker shit-eating mother of pearl sneaker boy wait for my armband wearing a jock around your neck to work the next day under your shirt dirt boot mark on your back long needles stuck in the tits underwearhole in the face disgrace love to wear your dogplates tied to the streetlamp cock hanging out boys laughing drink the water from the pool eat my balls extra hair asshole hair bruised let him loose choke swallow spit ram it down double over push down on back of neck engineer boots heavy rubber soles facelight steady eyes make him clean it up whip sounds beat up sounds heavy pain in the heart sounds boy begging sounds metal lock sounds sounds sounds of giving in of turning in hour time to me I do what I please ready to please to ease it in and out

Face

To get out of the face
On the endless ramps and trace

The ins and outs of seawater
On sand, then on wood, a motor

Is heard in the loose morning
Like the behind of a star mooring

In a yellow cotton-sheet bed.
At best you will wake up dead

Electric scissors accidentally in hand
Phone off the hook, a mystery man

With an opportunity to float for days
On end, broken off lakeside gaze

The static wooden village collapses
The mountain remains, glacier stains

The beauty marks of North Europe,
Mountains and glaciers like night and day

Are born for different reasons.
You epitomize the transitional seasons

And control by melting, or inter-facing
Your alloyed moods. This depressing

Need to grow up is really a static
Postage-due stamp. The true eclectic

Passes in-between the apparent weather
And emerges, a wraith, darker and wetter

Than the Alpine sunny musical village
Which elects him mayor. His secret rage

Provokes the village folk to convert,
But so much gook pours out of their shirts

They are abandoned in the treeless, seamless night
Knocking around without understanding their plight.

A cursory crimson rush of delight
Breaks the Mind barrier, old man's sight

Adjusts to all the phases of feeling
His own bad moves will send him reeling

Past the Open, the Messy, into a room
Cluttered again by knick-knacks that consume

The extra, the excessive light like blackholes
That burn light to create a smooth mixing bowl

Seducing your light hand
To touch and wipe and round the dark land

If you were in a ship it would be the same.
The gods are living in your arm. A tame

Half-swan, half-puff-of-smoke directs
By touch and intuition the boat past specks

So that even in the Ocean, the effect
Is always of riding through a Channel.

Old Testament Coloring Book

Turns into New Testament Coloring Book.
A dense manila sky surrounds the look
Of God. His eyes done in a tender pink
With Daniel's lions standing on the curve

Of sea and sky, the orange revolving tails
Auraed by brown; a squat building begins
The town of Jerusalem; dollar-bill palm leaves
Seen next to a hillside tent whose iron pegs

Stand out like silver notes printed on a page
Of popular sheet music, all the rage
In London Paris Amsterdam. A space
Begins to open, lovingly erase

The crowd scenes from the forehead of the Lord
Now left alone in his own tiny boat
He's going up to that rock to hit his head
Against his fist pressed up to the rock.

The hot black discolored tears are falling
Each weighed down Jupiter rocks with special weights
In the plutonic night, the purple night.
From pre-history to outer space the fright

Zig-zagging out around his hands and feet
Repeats its lightning strike pattern. The street
Speeds up then stops in front of Mary's house.
Dressed all in stripes. Her furniture devout.

Bending over the Lord's feet her telendrical hair
Handkerchiefs the outlines of feet and chair
Night fills one of the four square window panes
And Abyssinian holy beasts are sketched

With wings and tails and claws in the woodwork.
Now slowly the pages begin to jerk
And squeak. Old, dangerous amusement rides.
The soldiers with their plumes are at the door,

Their crimson throats are open with wisecracks.
A gold spear point flies off. Brilliant tracks
Of the Star of David in the white sky.
Skin-tone angels interchangeably flowing.

The Heavenly City is not pictured.
A long night is captured in the rough knee
Jabbing our pale vision. Now rough
Sun scours the ears of the bystanders. Enough

Emotion and color is generated
To dispense with the lines and the format.
You see three things: Noah's ark in the ceiling,
David's sheep on the porch and—not sleeping—

Christ on his way to heaven over the valley.
A voice gramophones through the broken tree.

The Second Anniversary of Christianity

On Paris/New York flight read Aquinas.
Return to Paris standing at Notre Dame
High Mass, something is going on, the Mass
Is in color, a priest is in a flame
Or rather behind a fence of candles.
Light change. Go outside into gray dove air
My best friend is with me, in her sandals
She walks me out the door, there are no stairs
No ding-dongs mix the heart with two parts water.
Each statue in its place, concrete puddles
Hold the horses and boot-pairs to the ground.
The exiting listeners are grouped in muddles.

Lonely days, lonely nights. I get your number
And arrange a meeting. The books are stocked
In a no-memory room, the zoom and whirr
Are soundproofed out, the green gray trees are knocked
Against the sky, you hate the earth, my dad
Is shredded by the lawnmower and green
Newspapers form a kind of lawn, the bad
Marble boys build a tomb. Now in the clean
Sanity Ward I wanted you to replace
His average face with your cloud-particle beard
And try to erase piece by piece my face
My clothes my feet. The next year disappeared.

You give me the run-around. All jobs are odd.
The different streets named after saints are mixed
In with secular parks. The whitest clod
Of earth produces the brownest tree. I missed the boat
And find myself on wooden cabin seat.
Sharp bird continuum. The dark is cold.
Sees her first patron saint then tries to kill
Herself, no cause/effect, light candle, build
A greeting card archway to outer space.
Inside her face is the face of a nun,
Inside the nun, a gun. A final trace
Of thinking fills the year with sun/moon peace.

2.

We can't seem to get off the ground together.
The weather is not divided into seasons.
Our wood beds join at the head; sounds in the feather
(Blackbird feathers) sky transpose to reasons
—PR Spanish—for us to split apart.
Then you shave your balsa wood head and pop pills,
Diamond bumps reapportion Mind, you start
Stick drawings of two men living in the hills.
One is water. One is fire. The air
Is most human, swirling without opinion
Around the fire tower, around the stairs,
Around the black-eyed bug on dandelion.

Each summer, a new feather to your wing
Extra voltage to your crown, strobing around
A resurrected head. The joy of singing
Leads imperfectly to tape deck, sonar,
Stereo equipment. The instruments
Wood string and reed simulate stomach pond
Deeply richly absent of Mind content.
Content to sit and watch your spreading hand
Band out from violet to brown, the land
Involuntarily powerful, to watch
And then connect the dots, a one-shot span
That suddenly constructs an Angel-Man.

Back in the tree, the boy is made of bone.
His eyes, flick flick, starling wings all over the valley
Take in Court House, King's College statue dome.
No words today, the cars are a mantra
Circulating the people from the houses.
Old lady watches in her emerald eyes
The image-reversal of no-longer spouse
Profiled in station wagon exhaust skies.
I like to walk to the corner with you.
In the basement we put on waxy high heels
In the attic, priest's sheets. Terrible blue—
Walking down the hall this is how mother feels.

If I can love a building I can love you.
It proves untrue, the morning starts to unravel.
I have not read most of the Old Testament.
No one close to me has died, on the swivel
Chair revolving like Earth see more sunlight
Each time, from low to medium high heat
The upsurge heat gets rid of a bumpy night
But the scene doesn't breathe as expected.
The brain is a beautiful Angola stamp.
Stuck on. Deeper than caring is not caring.
Deeper than Map, irresolute maker of map.
A hand-holding postcard, my way of giving.

Mixed Feelings

Again
have to admit to (stars) (cups)
warm feeling to you
who I am afraid of
because You are young
filled with lies hate
blaming the wrong person
when it is you
who are missing in action
this maya
could turn (the dragon's teeth)
against me But I know better,
and mixed in, I see you
in grass haze, unusually long day,
wearing a girl's face
being too concerned with the Past
showing off your underwear
in complete Self
You are not ugly, but sometimes
not as darkly handsome
as I imagine when away from you
or looking outside-in
to the idea You
in question
I would like to convert you
to cure you of Irish need for children
and arbitrary disciplines
that only simulate true character
In the blurry eyes of the anemone
a secretion of our universe flows
and in your secret Self

all the necessary duties carried out
into a bleached-out sky
horizon
On your palm I see railroad tracks
leading into a small town
your happiness is here
there is a spot, antennae on houses,
where all your rivers lines compactly meet
in sweet shade from tree fences
your expansion and beauty muscle build
an Angel-Man,
your hand is beginning to flower
and green infuses the paler shades
you are on your way
I am the waver at the station, both stations,
going and coming, I have enough iron
to build you tracks and enough imagination
to fill in a green-blue sky
which you might forget to do in your desire to rush there
thinking you have left us behind
whose scrutable faces are the map
of the rest of your life. Get used to us.
As for me, blink blink, as for me.

Looking Forward

Two days go by
the first, electric white
in and around the trees
most contracted in white streets
you don't come by
the second closes in
possibilities screen out the faces
hot, humid weather
turning to showers by late afternoon
by late afternoon no trees no doors
high cliffs slice aside reliefs, hills,
and as a perpendicular line
intersects and passes through the circle
each one of my thoughts is eventually You
in a different aspect
ocean peninsula island
Here in your necklace of rouge skulls
here in a kind of hatha-yoga floating routine
elbows knees positioned to make a Fish
the waves barely hitting your skimming stomach
the blue fire
circulating over and over in my own system
a biofeedback model
a new look at loneliness
And yet you prefer this harbor
to the clatter of the wrong ones
Knee-deep in the water
fisherman's boots
the light light part-moon
in gorgeous blue early morning sky
By gorgeous I mean coming

I mean transparent, vulnerable
with no clothes on
looking you cautiously in the eye
where it all happens
the fish-catching
the rocks monsterizing in deep dark
the tiny line of thought
passing out from the fisherman
his cold curvature forehead
into spaces
no family
no theory of natural selection
no blues no silvers
no noises no songs
just passing along
as sheep into dawn
the object not to catch a fish
seen now as a weight on the line
but to feel in the line-velocity
a certain tug
like the tug of a lady firefly
expressed in blimps of orange fire
revolving expressively on the leaf platform
her immaculate wish to come
by having him come to her.